1

CONTENTS

Introduction

This book is designed to make simple suggestions that will help you lose the weight. Once you start living healthy, this will be a lifestyle change. I use the word "diet" loosely in this book. This isn't a set program, and there isn't some magical pill you can take twice a day to give you the body you so desperately desire. It takes a ton of hard work, dedication, motivation, and drive. You won't wake up one morning with a new body. You have to put the time and effort in to get the results you want.

I tried many fad diets, Weight Watchers, and even weight-loss clinics, and none of them worked for me or they did temporarily. I got tired of always counting points or getting a shot or taking the pills. I wanted the easy fix. I came to realize it DOESN'T EXIST! I ALWAYS gained the weight back! There is only one way to live a healthy lifestyle, and the key is to move more and eat less! This is not a book where I tell you how many calories you can have in a day or how much exercise you have to do. This is a book that will hopefully get you in the mindset that you CAN lose the weight. I have listed tips and tricks in this book that will help you along your personal journey, and these have worked for me. I have been successful in losing over 80 pounds with the help of these simple suggestions. I don't deny myself anything, but I use common sense when making choices. I always eat when I am hungry, stop when I am full. Move more and eat less.

Who am I?

Let's be honest. There's nothing special about me. I don't have a degree in nutrition. I have not competed in any fitness competitions. I am not a personal trainer. There's absolutely nothing that connects me to the fitness world. But I do have life experiences that, if you are reading this book, you can probably relate to. I have been classified as morbidly obese, and I have had my fair share of struggles with peaks and valleys. I have been made fun of as the big girl. I have gone into clothing stores where I couldn't wear their largest size. I have gotten winded walking up a flight of stairs and thought it was a lost cause to walk up the next two flights so I found the elevator instead. I have been there, and I understand the struggle! I was tired of all the people who were naturally thin writing books about how to lose weight and the muscular personal trainers who would try to motivate me, with me knowing that they haven't been overweight a single day of their life. I needed something real, someone like me who had been in my shoes, who felt the feelings of despair that I was feeling. I get it. I understand. That is why I decided to take a leap of faith and be the voice of reason for people who were going through similar situations. I want you to know that I understand the thoughts and emotions that are in your head. I know the feeling of hopelessness and despair. I know what it's like trying to hide the pain I feel when I simply just want to look normal and feel like everyone else. I know what it's like to be out in public and get the looks from people, especially the skinny ones. In the mall I would avoid walking past Victoria's Secret for the simple fact that it made me feel bad. I know what it's like to not be able to make up my mind on what I want to eat, so I would just break down and buy them both to eat. There are so many instances that I had these feelings. I get it. This book skims the surface of my personal story, but it gives tips and tricks that I personally used to help lose the weight and to keep it off. I want you to be happy, healthy, and free - free from your personal torment. You are your biggest critic. Slow down. Examine your life. What is important to you? If losing the weight is important (I am assuming it is because you are reading this book), then take control. Take back the life you were given and quit wasting it. You have so much potential to be great, and you are holding yourself back. Give it your all. Don't make excuses anymore! If you fully invest in yourself, other things will follow.

I am here to tell you, you are not alone. You are worthy of love and so much more! Especially love for yourself. I want you to feel good mentally, physically, emotionally. I want you to love the skin you are in, and I want you to build confidence that I know you have deep within yourself. There's a small voice that knows your worth, and that needs to be found. That voice might be hidden, but it's there. You are strong. You are worth it!

Why are you overweight?

There is a reason you have problems with weight. You need to figure out the reason and address it. My problem was I was grieving, and food gave me the comfort I needed in order to feel better. I liked the taste of food. I would get a temporary high from enjoying good food, then I would feel bad because I ate too much, then I would eat to feel better. Food was my addiction. It was my feel-good drug of choice that ultimately only made me feel bad.

Many people are emotional eaters, some people just like the taste of food and have problems with portion control, and others eat certain things out of convenience. No matter the reason, figure it out and get it under control. Once you know the reason, it's easier to control the problem.

I encourage you to figure out what makes your brain tick and why you feel the need to eat certain things. You should be eating to live, not living to eat.

Figure out your "WHY?"

Why do you want to lose the weight? For me, I wanted to be healthy so I can watch my children grow. My dad passed away too early, and I feel as if he is missing out on a huge part of my life. He died of a heart attack at the age of 61. He always said, "One day I will be dead and gone and you will need to take care of your mother." He said this to me all the time. I am not sure if he genuinely knew he was going to die or if he was trying to mentally prepare me just in case, but it happened. This is the hand I've been dealt. So I can learn from it or I can live in a daily struggle with the mindset of, "What if?" I choose to learn from it, and I believe that is what he would have wanted for me. With him passing away at, in my opinion, an early age, I know that I do not want to leave my children in the same situation. I would like to be around to enjoy their adulthood. This is what drives me. This is ultimately MY "why." The route I was going wasn't working. I was overweight and tired all the time! That is no life to live.

Many reasons pushed me to where I wanted to lose the weight. How I felt on the inside was another major reason. I was tired and my back hurt all day, every day. I didn't want to go anywhere or do anything because I was embarrassed of how I looked. I was the big girl and I knew it. Not to mention my health was suffering. I constantly felt as if I would pass out from being out of breath or my heart would explode when I climbed up a flight of stairs. I started to ask myself, "what's more important to me, the food I was eating or how I felt."

Your reason might be different from mine, but I encourage you to figure out your "why." This will be the key factor in what drives you to reach your goals. Your "why" will be the remaining factor when everything else doesn't seem as important when you are tired and frustrated.

Find what motivates you. It can be anything from a goal pair of jeans, to being able to walk up the stairs without being winded, to being a better, more involved parent, to getting something that you are working toward, to having a better sex life. There can be many avenues of motivation. You just need to find yours. What drives you? Figure out your "why!"

Quit Making Excuses!

I was the worst at making excuses! I would always tell myself that I would start my diet "tomorrow." I was always too tired to start right away. Or I used the excuse, "I will start Monday." Then Monday would roll around and I would continue to make excuses!

One of my favorite excuses was that I had too many good things in the fridge. "Let me eat everything I have and then I can get serious about it." I would tell myself I would start after all of the sweets were gone. Or I would tell myself I needed one last meal of the things I wanted to eat before I got serious.

Why do so many of us do this? People don't want to get out of their comfort zone. We think of all the things that we think we will have to give up and delicious foods we will have to sacrifice or not eat. We are creatures of habit. We have our daily routines and are comfortable just surviving. I don't want to just survive. I want to thrive. I want to be my own voice of reason and be in control of the things that I have let control me for so long.

I needed someone to look me in the eye and tell me to get serious! Quit making excuses! Your life will NEVER change if you don't do something about it now! We are only given a set number of days on this Earth. Would you rather live those days being miserable, having a daily struggle with yourself, or would you rather take the bull by the horns, get serious, and learn to love the skin you are in? Nobody is going to do the work for you. YOU have to do it. I have said this time and time again: YOU are your own worst enemy!

Consistency

Consistency is imperative to weight loss! It is an everyday, nonstop commitment to living a healthy lifestyle. Making lasting changes in your own life, no matter how minor or how drastic, will put you in the right direction to a new, thinner you. Losing weight is not a race! Many people put a time frame on how much weight they want to lose in a designated amount of time. You are doing it wrong! It is great to set goals and I strongly recommend setting goals, but as long as the inches are coming off, you are succeeding in the ultimate goal, which is losing the weight and making the changes to live a better life. Success doesn't come from what you do occasionally. It comes from what you do consistently. With this plan you don't have to feel as if it's the end of the world. It is a lifestyle change. If you feel the need to have something sweet, do it, but only in small doses every now and then. Moderation is key!

Forgiveness

Let me throw this out there - you are NOT perfect! I am not perfect! We make mistakes. We are human! We will have moments of weakness, and at times we will give in to temptation. That is okay! Forgive yourself and move on! Tomorrow is another day and a new beginning. Start fresh and make it count. You can't dwell on the past. You can only move forward.

In the past, I would sometimes give in to temptation, and I still do from time to time. But I have learned the mindset - is this food really worth it? My answer is almost always no. Then I talk myself out of it. I know that I can consume the extra calories, but me fitting into a smaller size is more important than the temporary pleasure I would feel with having something sweet. Sweets are my kryptonite! Or I think to myself, "Do I feel like working out to work off those extra calories I just consumed?" That answer is almost always NO. Working out is my least favorite thing to do. I would rather not eat it than to work out.

When I was overweight, I felt the need to have dessert after every single meal. I sometimes planned my meals around my desserts! I eventually realized that I was going about it all wrong. Just because I can, doesn't always mean I should. That is when you have to take other things into consideration and decide what is the most important to you. Is it temporary pleasure? YES! It only feels good in the moment. Have you ever heard the saying, "Sweet moment on the lips, but a lifetime on the hips"? This is so true! It is hard to work off those temporary pleasures! I know my goals. I listed them at the beginning of the book. Will that temporary pleasure get me there? NO! I want to be healthy, look good, and feel great! Dessert after every single meal isn't realistic when you are wanting to lose weight. I am not saying that you can't EVER have those pleasures. But they need to be planned in advance and factored in BEFORE you get there. Do your homework. Try to always know ahead of time what you plan to order. It sounds weird, but trust me. It works!

Forgive yourself, but don't abuse your own forgiveness. Don't use this as an excuse to always give in and eat like crap. Still hold yourself accountable. This shouldn't be a crutch, and it should only rarely happen. If it is happening more often than not, you really need to examine what you are doing and why you are doing it.

Meals

Having larger meals is a thing of the past. Portion size is EVERYTHING! I recommend eating small portions 5-8 times a day - not an entire four-course meal, just something small. For example, eat a handful of nuts and a piece of fruit for a snack, or for a meal grilled chicken with some vegetables. Mix it up and make it fun. You need to feed your metabolism. Many people make the mistake of only eating large meals (breakfast, lunch, and dinner) with multiple hours in between those meals. By the time the next meal time arrives, you are starving and by then you have probably already scoped out something you can graze on, something salty, or something sweet. Or they feel as if they are starving, so portion size is out the window. This is one of the biggest downfalls of a typical diet. You can still have breakfast, lunch, and dinner, but you will need to spread it out and you will need to consume a fraction of what you used to. It's all about portion control and eating when you are hungry and stopping when you are full. Listen to your body! It will tell you when it's full, and once you realize what being full feels like, it will be easier to stop yourself. Sometimes when I am eating something so tasteful, I do not want to stop eating. I just want one more bite because it tastes so good! That is where you will need to learn willpower. You have to be able to tell yourself to stop no matter how good it is! That temporary pleasure of having something delicious in your mouth goes away in 1-2 minutes, but it takes a lot of time for it to actually leave your body, and the effects, depending on what it is, might last even longer. If you stop when you are full, you could put the remaining food in a to-go box and enjoy it a different time. Just spread out the time between eating it. It's all about portion control!

Sometimes when life gets in the way, you might skip a meal. Skipping a meal is a huge mistake! Skipping a meal makes your body go into starvation mode. Your body gets confused and starts storing all the excess calories that would typically be expended because it doesn't know when it will be able to eat again. If you eat 5-8 times a day, something small every 1-2 hours, your body doesn't go into hibernation mode and those excess calories will be expended. Skipping a meal is one of the worst things you can do. It sets you up for failure.

Meal prep is an excellent way to plan ahead. Overall it will save you time, money, and cut down on the amount of questions about what you will eat next. If you work or spend time away from home, meal prepping is the way to go. You can easily keep track of calories, and it saves time. I buy my meal prep storage containers online. Each container has three dividers with a lid - one for meat and two vegetables or a vegetable and fruit. I weigh everything on a food scale and look up the number of calories. Then I take a sticky note and label each one. I do this once a week for my husband and me. I call it my "easy readys." I only spend one day (usually Sunday afternoon) preparing a couple of meals - usually different types of chicken - but I change it up a bit with steak, fish, and the occasional pork chop. You will want to mix it up a bit so it doesn't get monotonous. I usually prepare 10 total - one for each of us, for lunch, every day of the week Monday through Friday - and they are good for the entire week. Grabbing these meals from the refrigerator allows us to plan ahead and saves time preparing meals every day. It also allows us to shop in bulk, so that saves money! Who doesn't like to save time and money? I know I do! If you struggle for recipes, you can always find healthy, delicious meals on the internet.

Another way to plan ahead and save time and money is to use a slow cooker. This is great for dinners. You can buy in bulk, which saves money! You will want to separate each meal and freeze what you aren't planning on using right away. The day before you decide you want that certain meal, thaw it out the night before and put it in the slow cooker during the day. That way when you get home, you have a hot and ready meal that will look like and taste like you spent hours on it! This will also save you time in the evenings! You can have a sit-down meal waiting to be enjoyed! This will give you more time to spend with your loved ones or even alone reading a good book! If you need recipes, you can look online or find some in a magazine or a book. Recipes can be found almost anywhere!

Listen to Your Body

You need to listen to your body and not your taste buds. Your body will tell you when you are full. That is when you need to stop eating. When sitting down to eat, at least for a while until you recognize the feeling of full, I would suggest eating at the table with no distractions- No TV, no cellphone, and no electronic devices. Drink 8-16 ounces of water and wait 5 minutes, then begin to eat. Take small bites and chew very well. Take your time and listen to what your body is telling you. You will start to feel full and when you have that feeling- STOP!! Even if your food is absolutely delicious, make yourself STOP! This is the key to losing weight without dieting! Eat when you are hungry, stop when you are full. Drink your water.

It sounds crazy, but I feel full around 5-7 bites. When beginning to dine- I drink my 8-16 ounces of water, wait my 5 minutes, I eat my 5-7 bites, my body starts to feel full, and I stop!

Stopping is crucial! You might think that I am starving, but trust me, I am not. Do you know why? Because I eat when I am hungry, I stop when I am full. We need to change the mindset revolving around food. We don't have to have a four-course meal with appetizer, soup, entrée, and dessert. We should be consuming a fraction of that amount of food. Another thing to consider is sometimes humans confuse hunger pangs with thirst. You may think you are hungry, when in fact, you are thirsty. Drinking that water before you eat will help you determine the difference.

When eating you should always aim to eat proteins first, vegetables second, fruits third, then carbs and fats. Proteins will make you feel fuller longer, so you will eat less. You will want to consume chicken, fish, and turkey because these are your leaner protein choices. Vegetables are second because you they have beneficial nutrients your body needs. Try to consume green leafy veggies such as broccoli, spinach, asparagus, and brussels sprouts because these are packed full of nutrients. Fruits should be third on your list because they have vitamins your body needs. Lastly you should consume carbs and fats.

You need to think of your body as a car. Cars need maintenance, need to be lubricated, tuned up, and each part of that machine has a function, whether it be nuts and bolts that hold the machine together or fluids that travel in the machine that keep it lubricated. It doesn't matter if you are a fast sports car or if you are a classic. We want our bodies to perform at the top notch. We must treat it right and take care of it. Eat the foods that will help your body thrive and give you energy. Stay away from junk food. Junk food is the equivalent of putting sugar in your gas tank. Drink your water. This will help lubricate your joints and help your digestion tract. Go to the doctor regularly for checkups, just like a tune-up. Fuel your body. Focus on nourishing your body instead of depriving it. Give it the nutrients you need in order to run properly. This is the same as putting fuel into a car.

Moderation

Moderation can be defined as the avoidance of excess or extremes. Moderation needs to be in your everyday vocabulary when making this lifestyle change. Every food can be consumed every now and again in moderation. This includes salty, sweet, red meats, and fried foods. Even alcohol can be consumed in small quantities. Doing without or denying yourself indulgences from time to time is why some people tend to fail. They fall off the wagon and get discouraged, never returning and regretting choices made. The weight never comes off and regret sets in. A small amount of time passes and you are in the same boat you started in.

I am a firm believer that you can have your guilty pleasures, but do it wisely. Make up for those extra calories with exercise, or make sure you take the caloric count into account when figuring your other foods out for the day. I believe in planning ahead, and by doing this, this will allow you to have those guilty pleasures without consuming too many empty calories.

Calories and Pounds

Calories are the energy in food. Your body demands energy and uses the calories from food to function. The calories you consume are either converted into physical energy or stored within your body as fat. These stored calories will remain in your body as fat unless you use them. This can be done either by diet, where you reduce your caloric intake so that your body must draw on reserves for energy, or by exercising or increasing your physical activity so that you burn more calories.

To lose one pound a week, you need to achieve a 3,500-calorie deficit. The reason dieting is more effective than exercise is because it is easier to cut out a few hundred calories per day as compared to working out where it takes a ton of energy to create a 500- to 1,000-calorie deficit throughout the week. So to lose one pound a week, you could do a daily workout that burns 500 calories.

(500 calories X 7 Days a week = 3500 Calories (1 Pound))

Burning about 1,000 extra calories per day through exercise would help you lose two pounds a week.

(1,000 calories X 7 Days a week= 7,000 calories (2 Pounds))

It would be much easier to combine diet with exercise. You could choose low-calorie, high-nutrient foods along with a small amount of daily exercise and lose the weight more easily as compared to just doing one or the other. Remember to sweat and get your heart rate up while exercising!

Water

If you want to lose weight, you must drink water, and lots of it. A good rule of thumb is to drink half your body weight in ounces of water. For example, if you weigh 200 pounds, you need to at least drink 100 ounces of water. Water comprises 60 percent of your body. It flushes out toxins, lubricates your joints, reduces fatigue, maintains regularity, improves skin complexion, prevents cramps, and boosts your immune system. If you want to step it up a notch, drink cold water. When drinking cold water, your body temperature will decrease, causing your body to burn more calories and work much harder trying to warm itself back up. One 16-ounce glass of cold water can burn approximately 17.5 calories.

If you need flavor in your water, add some lemon. Lemon can aid in digestion and detoxification, give you additional vitamin C, boost your energy, put you in a better mental state, heal the body, rejuvenate the skin, and is also a natural diuretic that can help relieve bloating and help you lose water weight. Lemon can be added to cold or hot water and can offer medicinal values by cleansing the body, improving digestion, and stimulating the liver. Lemon water can also help reduce the amount of uric acid in joints, which can help eliminate joint pain.

If you are strength training or doing aerobic exercise, consider drinking more water. Water is a very good thing.

Drink 8-16 ounces of water and wait 5 minutes BEFORE eating any meal. This will help you from over eating, help your body feel fuller faster, and it will also help your water intake for the day. I would say this is the second most important rule next to portion control (which is the next section we will be discussing.)

Do not drink your calories! There are hundreds of types of drinks out there. Many drinks are loaded with sugar, which can be high in calories, and you probably don't even realize it. Soft drinks contain a crazy amount of sugar and artificial flavorings that are packed full of empty calories! I was the worst about drinking sodas. I would say it was a huge contributor to my weight gain. I was almost addicted to it, because I drank it with every meal and in between meals. I was guilty of getting that 44-ounce Coke ICEE from the local gas station, which on average can be anywhere between 200 and 300 calories in ONE drink! If you are allowing yourself 1,200 calories, that is ¼ of you daily caloric intake! I was either oblivious or didn't care, but I am here to tell you - CARE! Don't be lazy. Know what you are putting into your body!

Juices are also loaded with empty calories. Most juices have the same amount of calories as sodas! Don't be fooled by packaging and marketing. Many large corporations use marketing and colorful packaging to confuse the public, making them think that these fruit juice drinks are good for them. Phrases such as "no artificial flavorings" or "100 percent fruit juice" can be very misleading. These products are not good for you! If you want 100 percent fruit juice, eat a piece of fruit, not some soda they have labeled 100 percent fruit juice! Juices often have preservatives that allow them to sit on a shelf longer. Don't be naive and put these chemicals into your body. Read the labels on the packaging, and pay attention to sugars and calories.

When it comes to coffee and delicious coffee drinks, coffee has some health benefits. It can improve energy levels and make you feel less tired because of the caffeine in it. Caffeine is a stimulant that can suppress your appetite. Caffeine can increase fat burning in the body and boost your metabolism. Coffee contains several important nutrients including riboflavin, magnesium, pantothenic acid, potassium and niacin. Coffee might also protect you or lower your risk against multiple diseases including cancer, Parkinson's disease, Alzheimer's disease, and type 2 diabetes. Some call it the "elixir of life." There are many health benefits to coffee. However, when you add sugar and creamer into your coffee, this transforms the "elixir of life" into a high-calorie drink, which in turn will help you pack on the pounds. The same goes with the frozen coffee drinks or specialty drinks. Yes, these are delicious, but these are also loaded with sugar and are high in calories, so be aware of what you are consuming!

Portion Size

In today's society, portion sizes are out of control. If you are eating at a restaurant, portion sizes are three or four times larger than they need to be. Why is this? It's because people are attracted to the amount of food for the price. We live in a world where we have been trained to think bigger is better. So restaurants give you huge portions, which in turn makes you eat three or four times more than you actually need. This causes a weight gain. When eating out, try splitting your meal with someone. This will cut down on cost and the amount of food in front of you. Most restaurants will actually split the meal for you in the back if you ask. Another suggestion would be to ask for a to-go box with your food. Once your food is delivered, put half of your meal in the to-go box so you don't overeat. You can take the leftovers to eat for another meal, which will also save you money. Drinking water also allows you to save money, and it helps you get your daily amount of water in. I have a family of five. Setting a good example by drinking water and requiring my children to drink water saves my bank account at least 10-15 bucks every meal when eating out. It also teaches my children the importance of drinking water.

When I was growing up, I was taught to eat everything on your plate. "Only take what you will eat," and you were required to finish eating everything you took. This has affected my mindset as an adult. "Don't be wasteful, and always finish what's on your plate!" This is another factor that has attributed to my weight gain. When cooking at home, I serve all our meals on smaller plates. It looks like a lot of food, but in reality, it's much less than a dinner plate and truthfully, it's all you really need. Cutting down on portion sizes is the single most important factor that has helped my weight loss. I was out of control with my eating, and I didn't even realize it at the time.

Read Labels!

I can't emphasize enough to read your labels! Know what you are cooking, buying, and ordering! With today's technology there is no excuse to live in a bubble. The information is out there, and if it's not on the back of the package I can almost guarantee it can be found on the internet. Don't be lazy. That is what put you in this situation to begin with! Do the work! Once you read the label, you can make an educated decision for yourself if you should really be consuming the product. Check out serving size, calories, carbs, proteins, fiber, fats, and sugars. Take it all into account and then decide. I am not here to tell you what you can and can't eat. I am simply here to tell you what worked for me and give you a little insight on the things you might or might not already know. Knowledge is power! Read that label!

The Dreaded Scale

We all worry about the scale, but why? I weigh myself every single morning. I wake up, use the restroom, strip off all my clothes, then climb on the scale only to be disappointed. That sets the tone for my entire day. Why do I do this? Is it because I want to weigh less? YES YES YES! But is that really my ultimate goal? The answer is NO! My ultimate goal is to feel better, be healthy, look good in the skin I am in, and to wear a smaller size clothes or for my clothes to fit better. I want to play with my kids without getting tired or even walk up a flight of stairs without getting winded.

The scale is ultimately my enemy! But why?

This is why:

One pound of fat is the same as one pound of lean muscle, but visibly they look very different. Muscle is much denser, takes up less space, and has a firm touch, as compared to one pound of fat, which is much larger, takes up a larger amount of space, and is squishy to the touch.

Here is an example:

1 Apple
Represents 1 pound
of lean muscle

32 Marshmallows
Represents 1 pound
of fat

The apple that represents muscle is much denser and displays a firm tone. It is hard to the touch and can't be squeezed. It has a smooth appearance. Now compare that same apple to the 32 marshmallows that represent the fat. The marshmallows are larger, take up more space, and are fluffier. When touched, they can be squeezed and are bumpy in appearance that, when lumped together, can resemble cellulite from fat.

Below is a picture that displays two people who weigh exactly the same, but as you can see, they look very different!

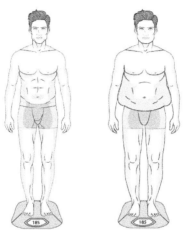

Person with Muscle   **Person with Fat**

These two people weigh the same, but visibly they look very different! The scale only measures weight, not success.

If choosing to weigh yourself, I recommend doing it once a week at the same time each week. You can do it every day. Just know that weight can fluctuate anywhere from 2-4 pounds on any given day. Your sodium intake should be kept to a minimum for this reason! Large amounts of sodium can show huge increases on a scale!

Keeping a Blog

Holding yourself accountable is very important. I would recommend starting a blog or keeping a diary. A blog would allow you to get support from family and friends. This is what I did. I posted everything from daily struggles, to my meals, pictures, measurements, and workouts. As I progressed I was able to post before and after pictures. I believe my blog motivated me more than anything because it held me accountable to my actions and what I was eating. It allowed my family and friends to give me support and encouragement when I needed it the most. This helped me stay on track, and it allowed me to be an inspiration to others.

Keeping a diary is more for people who don't necessarily need the encouragement of others but would like to keep track of where they started and how they felt while they were doing it. I benefited more from a social blog than a diary simply because I needed the encouragement. There's no wrong or right way to do it. It just depends on what you personally need. A diary allows you to keep track of your measurements, pictures, how you felt on a daily/hourly basis, and you can also keep tabs on things that are working versus things that aren't. Don't get the diary confused with the food journal. These are two different things but can be combined if you wanted.

Food Journal

A food journal allows you to keep track of everything you are putting in your mouth. If you don't understand why you are gaining the weight, the food journal really puts into perspective everything you are eating and drinking. The food journal is typically broken down by breakfast, lunch, and dinner, with a possible snack, and you can label by the type of food you are eating, serving size, and calorie count. When eating 5-8 times a day, adjust your food journal to fit your needs. You can also keep track of the amount of water you are drinking. You can use it to improve your health and make changes to your diet. The food journal makes you accountable to yourself. Just remember if you consume it, even if it's only a bite, you write it down! Don't cheat yourself!

Setting Goals

It is important to set goals for yourself. I suggest making a 90-day goal, but set smaller goals within that 90-day time frame. Be realistic when making these goals. There's nothing more disappointing than working hard, then not hitting your goal. Remember, a healthy weight loss will be around two pounds a week. When I was losing weight, my 90-day goal was to lose 24 pounds and to lose inches, because that's an average of two pounds a week for three months. I had set smaller goals for myself. Every week I was determined to lose at least the two pounds, but I would always shoot for more. But I would also set daily goals and sometimes even hourly goals.

My weekly goals were the two pounds and trying to shrink my waist, hips, thighs, and butt. I would weigh myself every week, take my measurements, and keep a blog about it. I would check to make sure I had stayed honest with myself on the daily goals and in my food journal. I knew if I did the work daily, the weekly goals would more than likely be hit.

My daily goals would be to stay strict to my diet, keep track of everything I consumed in my food journal, walk 15 minutes (if not more), get at least six hours of sleep, and to give at least one person a day a compliment. How hard is that? It's not. It's just holding myself accountable to do the things I said I was going to do.

My hourly goals were much easier to do because they were in my face and needing to be done right away. I would set an hourly goal and tell myself, "Next hour, I am going to walk up and down the flight of stairs in my office two times. I am going to measure the amount of food I will possibly be putting in my mouth." If I were home with my children, we would go for the 15-minute walk and take the dog. The hourly goals were easier for me because they were current.

If you do the things you say you are going to do, it will not only make it easy to reach your goals, but it also builds character. It makes you a person of your word and someone you can trust. It sets a good example for your children, and when people think of you, they will know that you are a trustworthy person simply because you followed through and did the things you said you were going to do.

Pictures and Measurements!

This is the only true way to tell if you are slimming down. The scale won't be as accurate. If you take measurements before you start your weight-loss journey and after a few weeks of remaining steady, you will be able to tell if you are making progress. Remember, consistency is key! Write your measurements down in your blog or diary so you can keep up with them. You will be amazed at your progress in just a couple of weeks.

You will also want to take pictures. When I first started, I took pictures of myself in a mirror with yoga pants and a sports bra. Today I can tell a major difference in the way I look. I often do a side by side and post it on my blog. If you aren't comfortable taking pictures without your shirt on, that's okay. I strongly recommend taking the pictures, even if it's just for yourself and comparison later.

Realization and Who Really Matters

I had a hard time finding full-body shots because I was never happy with the bottom half of my body so I would always crop it out, especially if I had planned to post on social media. I was embarrassed of how much weight I had gained. I finally realized that other people didn't care about me as much as I had originally thought. I was just the topic of conversation when my posts were to appear. Other than that, was I even thought about? After a while I finally decided that their opinions didn't matter and I would give them something to talk about. Their opinions of me didn't make or break me. Why did I even care what they thought? To be honest, I didn't even like them. Why the need for acceptance? I think everyone wants to be liked and everyone wants to be accepted. Once you learn to love yourself, you will realize it's all superficial anyway. Social media is a joke. It's the only place where you are friends online and ignore one another in person when you see each other. It's all about keeping up with the Joneses and who has the latest and greatest toy or biggest house. We spend countless hours ignoring the ones who truly matter - our family - for those who would ignore us on the street. When all is said and done, who would take the time to show up at your hospital bed or attend your funeral? Now those are your real friends! Those opinions matter, and those are the people we need to cling to for support.

Ignore the haters and the people that will bring you down. You will have some! We all do. Everyone will have an opinion about what you are doing and how you are doing it. Let me be the first to say- It's okay to unfriend and unfollow people. I have had to do it a ton, people get on my nerves with their opinions! If someone is not contributing to your success, chances are, they are part of your problem. People like to gossip and tell stories, it's natural sinful nature, but if it is affecting your mood and contributing negativity to your mindset- CUT THEM OFF! You don't need them!

Sleep

Sleep plays an important role in your physical and mental health, which ultimately attributes to your weight loss. It is recommended that you get between six and eight hours of sleep every night. People who get between six and eight hours of sleep are less likely be depressed, they have a better outlook on daily situations, they don't eat to stay awake, they tend to be healthier, and they have more motivation. Sleep allows your body time to recuperate from the day. It allows your body to repair cells, heal, and fight off infection. Sleep gives your heart a break and prevents cognitive issues. It allows you to be fully functioning throughout the day. It improves your memory, decision-making, reaction time, alertness, reasoning, and problem-solving.

Not getting enough sleep can make you irritable and weaken your immune system. You will tend to eat more or graze, be depressed, have a decreased sex drive, be more emotional, be forgetful, be a pessimistic, and ultimately you are more likely to just have a bad attitude. Your risk of diseases and cancer increases when you don't get enough sleep. And the chance of you being involved in a car accident increases because it can affect your response time.

Insomnia played a huge factor in my weight gain. I was grieving from the loss of my dad, and it prevented me from getting the adequate amount of sleep I needed to function. I finally had to force myself to go to the doctor to address the issue. Once I was able to sleep, I could control my eating habits more and it prevented me from snacking because I wasn't so tired throughout the day. Many people would be embarrassed because I had to go to the doctor to help my issue. We are not all the same. Different things affect people differently. Never be embarrassed of your situation. You need to address the problem or problems you have, or you will have roadblocks succeeding.

Mind, Body, and Spirit

Regardless of what you believe or what religion you are, you need to nurture your spirit, mind, and body. Take time out of the day to dedicate to yourself. I like to pray or meditate. It gives me a chance to regroup and talk to my Lord, Jesus Christ. It's peaceful, and when I am feeling overwhelmed it calms me. I feel like I can really focus and it gives me clarity. It helps me put into perspective the things that matter, the things that can be overlooked, and the things that aren't worth the attention. I enjoy the quiet, and it has a relaxing feel that soothes my mind and body.

If you aren't a spiritual person, just take time to be in the quiet with no distractions. Enjoy time alone to just breathe and exist. Let your worries go out the window and invest in yourself. When you are fully invested, that is when you can truly give 100 percent to others.

There's a direct correlation between mental health and physical health. If your mind isn't healthy, your body will suffer, and vice versa. The amount of sleep, foods we eat, and daily activities not only affect our physical health, but they also affect our mental health. Focus on your mental health first. This will allow you to fully commit, stay focused, and stay determined to reach your physical health goals.

Exercise

Exercise as much as possible! You should AT LEAST be designating 30 minutes a day at least three times a week to exercise! Are you sweating? If that answer is NO - repeat after me - I NEED TO SWEAT! Work out that heart! You need to take time out for yourself! There is no excuse not to take three days a week to exercise. This doesn't mean you have to sneak off to the gym away from your family to exercise! If you have that luxury and it works for you, then great! Go do it! I will encourage that all day long! But some people don't have the ability to get away. Involve your kids! Be the example! If you have smaller children, use their body weight to lift them. Older children will love the attention of being included. You can find all kinds of videos on www.youtube.com if you are stuck in the house or need ideas. If it's nice outside, take advantage of it! Go for a brisk walk and let your children ride their bikes, play a round of tag, hide-n-go-seek, or even old-school kick the can. Bring back those games we loved to play when we were a kid, and get your children away from their electronics. Build a memory. These are the type of things your children will remember. Leave your legacy! The possibilities are endless. Get creative with it! But you NEED to SWEAT! It is a MUST to lose weight and keep it off!

Why do we sweat? Sweating helps regulate body temperature and can also rid the body of heavy metals and toxins that can harm the body. Sweat has been known to boost endorphins that make you feel good. That's why after you get a good workout in, you feel great and you are in a better mood. It also helps control mood swings. Releasing that endorphin can help with depression and anxiety. A lot of people work out because it is a stress reliever. Sweating has been known to prevent colds and other illnesses or diseases, reduce injury time, and prevent muscle strain. Sweat can help clear up your skin. Sweat helps unclog your pores and releases built-up toxins that cause blemishes. Sweating protects your heart, increases circulation, and strengthens the cardiovascular system. It also boosts blood flow to skeletal muscles and can boost growth hormone production, which is the body's way of repairing itself. Sweating can boost a person's sex drive. When sweat is excreted, it carries certain pheromones with it. Overall, sweat does a body good and we can all benefit from a good sweat!

Remember, muscle burns more calories at rest than fat. It is important to be able to burn calories while you sleep. The more calories, the better! Every chance you get, you need to be exercising. I'd recommend taking the stairs, park in the farthest parking spot from the door, going for a walk, and go to the park as often as you can. Don't miss out on your surroundings! You must hustle for that muscle! Challenge your spouse to a push-up or sit-up contest. A little competition never hurt anyone. Burn those calories and get that heart rate up!

Adding exercise to any changes you have made to your diet will drastically cut down on the time it takes for you to see results! By combining these two elements you will be on your way to a happier and healthier you!

Never Deny Yourself Anything!

One reason these fad diets fail is because you have to completely do without something. For example, on the Atkins diet you have to eliminate most carbs. When doing this you will find that your body craves the things it has been denied. That is when people "fall off the wagon." It is simply a fad diet and it rarely lasts. Once you start eating carbs again, your body starts storing them because it went so long without. That's the reason for gaining weight back so quickly.

I am a firm believer in allowing yourself to have the things you want, but only in small doses. Use your common sense. If you eat a large slice of cheesecake after every meal, it's only common sense that you will gain weight. That's not what I am saying. What I am saying is live your life, but be smart about it. For example, if you are out to eat with a group of people and you want some cheesecake, order the cheesecake! But share it with your friends. Only have a couple of bites and give everyone some. Share! Sharing is caring!

Don't deny yourself the things you love because you are on a "diet." That's when you will fail. If you denied yourself every single time you wanted cheesecake, eventually you will eat that cheesecake, but maybe it would be a WHOLE cheesecake next time and not just a slice. There's no need to "fall off of your diet." This should be more of a lifestyle change where you make smart choices with food.

Find Your Purpose

Sometimes when people eat, it is merely out of boredom! This is why I say find your purpose! We all have our place in this world, and if you can figure out what makes you tick with the things you enjoy, it will be a fulfilling experience! Maybe you want to help others by volunteering your time. If you like animals, you could volunteer your time at an animal shelter. If you like sports, you could help coach a little league team or referee one. That would be a good calorie burner. If you want to help the environment, maybe you could help pick up trash on the side of the road. If you like to read, maybe you could help in a library or tutor a child who is having difficulties. If you have a hobby, maybe you could share your hobby with others and share your love for that hobby with someone. If you like children, maybe you could volunteer to be a "big brother" or "big sister" for underprivileged children. If you have extra funds to give away, you could donate money to a school or a family in need. You could help at a local church. Most churches need volunteers or members. You could help at a homeless shelter, serving food to the hungry. No matter what you like to do, figure out what makes you tick. Giving back to the community helps morale, boosts confidence, and helps others see you for who you really are!

The more time you are out doing activities and dedicating your time, the less time you are sitting in front of a TV or thinking about your next meal. You've got this! You are a loved individual with a purpose. You just need to figure out what it is and do it!

Don't Reward Yourself with Food!

People do this all the time, and I am even guilty of it! I would tell myself, "If I eat decent all week and follow through with my diet, we will go to my favorite restaurant this weekend." I am even guilty of doing it with my kids! I did this potty training my daughter. "If you pee in the potty, I will give you a couple of M&Ms." "You hit a home run. Let's go out for ice cream!" This only teaches children at an early age to be rewarded with food. We need to change our mindset. Instead of rewarding with food, why don't we participate in activities or do things with our kids that they would enjoy? Let's go skating, hiking, fishing, or to the playground! It doesn't have to cost money, and it would be memorable for your entire family! You can also reward yourself with smaller clothing! This can be fun once you start losing the weight! Nothing is more rewarding than to see your hard work pay off!

If food is your addiction, let's squash it!

That's like telling a drug user if he doesn't do drugs all week, that at the end of the week he can be rewarded with a "fix." It's the exact same thing. One is just legal. It is legal to be overweight, even if we are killing ourselves slowly doing it.

Preparing Yourself Mentally

If you are anything like me, every day is different. My husband, Wes, and I both work, and our children are involved in several activities after school. We are often on the go multiple times throughout the week. My advice is to prepare yourself the night before on the things you are doing the next day. Always plan meals in advance. If you are cooking for your family, plan ahead. Know portion sizes and calories per portion! If you are eating on the go, know ahead of time what you are planning to order. If you wait until you are starving to decide, trust me, you WILL overeat! In a world that is constantly on the go, be smart. Choose healthy!

Plan to get the proper amount of sleep each night. Make time for exercise, even if it is a walk around the neighborhood. Get it in your head that you will drink every ounce of water. Set out your vitamins so you don't forget to take them. Plan each and every aspect of your day, and follow though! You won't disappoint yourself if you plan ahead!

Alcohol

Limit the amount of alcohol you consume. I am a realist and I know most people drink, but during the time of weight loss it really needs to be cut to a minimum. Alcohol dehydrates you, and drinking adds empty calories on your daily caloric intake. For every drink you have, you will have to subtract something else from your diet (nutrients that you might need) or add extra exercise to counter the calories consumed. Alcohol also increases your appetite and impulsivity, so chances are you will eat substantially more while drinking. Keep in mind a 5-ounce glass of wine has around 150 calories, give or take, depending on the type of wine. A 1.5-ounce shot of vodka or 12 ounces of light beer will run you about 100 calories. Be sure to check nutritional values before consuming alcohol and be educated on your caloric intake! Always factor those in and be responsible! Know how much you are allowed to drink, and only drink your designated calories. This should be cut to the bare minimum and only be a once-in-a-while event!

Smoking

I debated whether to add smoking as a category in my book. I decided that it needed to be addressed because my book is about being a better version of yourself. If I left the category off without addressing it, I feel as if I would be doing you a disservice. Someone needs to tell you how it is, and I am not afraid of being the bad guy. If you are smoking, STOP! If you can quit cold turkey, QUIT! If you need to get gum or chew on toothpicks, do it! If you need to find a support group to help you stop, do it. If you have no other reason to quit, do it for your mother. I know as a mother, I would be greatly disappointed in my children if they picked up that nasty habit. Just imagine how proud your mother would be if you actually stopped. There's one thing we all have in common - our mothers. So if for no other reason, do it to make your mom proud.

I am a huge advocate for children, especially younger children who don't have a voice. If you are smoking and you have children, you really need to evaluate your priorities. Secondhand smoke can be just as unhealthy as personally lighting the cigarette and puffing on it. If you smoke, there is a greater chance your children will when they are older. Be the example! Break the cycle and stop the chain of events. You have the power to control the outcome. There are many things in life that are beyond your control. Smoking is NOT one of them. You have the power to stop. Now just do it. Take the steps and find out what works best for you. Imagine how much money you would save overall by simply saving the money you would spend on cigarettes.

Smoking is a deadly habit. It affects everything, from the way you breathe to how your skin looks. Smoking harms nearly every organ of the body and is the leading factor in most lung cancers. Smoking can also cause cardiovascular and respiratory diseases. There are many health risks associated with smoking, and there are so many reasons you should quit and not one single reason you should continue the habit, so if you are smoking, STOP!

Support System

Not having the support of someone can be detrimental in weight loss. My support system was my husband, Wes, and I was his. Together we have lost a combined weight of around 170 pounds to date, and there are no regrets. There have been so many days when I didn't feel like it or I just wanted to eat what I wanted to eat. Trust me - I understand and I get it. I have been there, but this is where having a strong support system came in handy for me. He helped encourage me on my hardest days when my biggest enemy was myself. But the support goes both ways. We are strong for each other, and while we were losing the weight there were days I was wrestling a piece of meat out of the lion's mouth, but I did what I had to do for him.

Having someone hold you accountable to your actions can really make a difference. It can be a family member, friend, church member, or even someone you met at the gym. Find someone with a common goal where you can help each other out, talk about your struggles, accomplishments, and praise each other. Celebrate goals together!

Watch the company you keep. People tend to pick up the same habits as the people they hang around. If you think about it, most of your friends possibly even look the same as you. I am not saying ditch your friends, but I am saying there needs to be a conversation about what your goals are, and if they are true friends they will support you and possibly even help you along your journey. Be the example! I had numerous people support me along the way, but I also had people who would make discouraging comments or tempt me in ways that would slow my progress. I found myself distancing myself from those bad influences. I will say it again, if they are TRUE friends, they will support you along the way. Cut the fat in more ways than one!

Parents on the Go

I know getting to the ball field, soccer field, or dance rehearsal can be hectic. You are picking up kids and rushing from one function to the next with very little time in between to worry about a meal. So you make a quick stop at a fast food restaurant or hit the concession stand because, let's be honest, it's easy! Most of the time, it's cheaper than making a meal for the family. What's better than the dollar menu? Hmm. Let's think about this. I can tell you - your health! Most everything on that dollar menu is processed, fried, greasy, etc. You are better than that!

Parents on the go probably have to plan ahead more than any other person because it's not just you. It's you and your entire family! I strongly emphasize meal prep! You can prep on Sunday evenings for grab and gos. You can grill chicken breasts and slice them so they're easy to eat from a baggie. Buy an insulated bag to keep things cool or hot. Put fresh veggies and fruits in baggies and hand those to your kids. They can eat when you get to the ball field. Pack a blanket for a picnic. Make it fun! Build a memory! It is healthier, and if you purchased in bulk you would be saving money. It might not be as much as the dollar menu, but your children will be eating healthy and you would also be consuming less calories than most everything on that dollar menu!

Remember, don't skip meals! Avoid skipping meals at all costs!

Apps

Use technology to your advantage! There are many avenues of technology you can explore when trying to lose weight. Cellphones are nothing more than mini computers that you carry everywhere. We need to use this to our advantage. There are several apps that can be used easily. There are a multitude of avenues you have, anywhere from nutrition facts, to pedometers, fitness challenges, calorie counters, workout trackers, sample workouts, distance trackers, and so on.

MyFitnessPal

One app I strongly recommend is MyFitnessPal. This app allows you to keep a food diary, set a calorie goal, keep track of your weight, and log everything you eat to help you stay on track. You can look up nutrition facts to almost any food and check restaurants' food nutrition to help you make healthy choices while dining out. You can also save your favorite meals! There's also a way to import recipes to get the nutritional stats, which can make it quick and easy. They have more than 6 million foods in their database. It's very user-friendly and a great resource to help you keep track of what you are consuming. Over time you will be able to see patterns in your habits. This will help you make adjustments when needed if you plateau or start to struggle. The creators of the app also included a way to scan barcodes of food products to add your nutrition facts easily. All you have to do is place the barcode inside the viewfinder in order to scan it, and it literally takes seconds!

I am not the best with technology, and I found this app to be easy to use and learn. It can be a little overwhelming at first, but once I started to play with it, I could see all the options it offered. In the diary you can flip back and forth between the days to see what you have eaten and to see how well you stayed within your calories. At the top of the screen, you will see your total caloric goal for the day. You can see the total number of calories you have eaten, a place that keeps track of your exercise, and how many calories you have remaining. It is very simple and straight to the point. It looks like this:

2,440 - 548 + 334 = 2,226

Goal - Food + Exercise =Remaining

You can log your weight and sync with other apps. This can be done automatically, cutting down on time. It also makes keeping track of water intake easy and is good for someone not wanting to physically keep track of calories in a notebook or journal.

Fitbit

Fitbit is dedicated to helping people lead more active lives. It has many options, from a watch-style tracker that you wear on your wrist, to a smaller tracker you can connect to your clothes. The trackers sync with the Fitbit app on your phone. A Fitbit is a great way to keep track of how much exercise you are doing. This app allows you note how much exercise you are getting to how much sleep you are sleeping. I like the Fitbit because you can include your friends. If a friend has a Fitbit you can keep track of how much or how little they are doing. You can do challenges with each other and it helps you stay connected. You can also keep track of your weight loss. Some Fitbits can monitor heart rate, and it automatically syncs with the app on your phone. There is a section dedicated to heart rate that displays your resting heart rate and how much it fluctuates each day.

You can set your settings on your Fitbit to how many steps you want to take within the hour. If you haven't reached your goal, your Fitbit will buzz and tell you that you are short that amount of steps for your hourly goal. This will require you to get up and take those steps. It's genius. There is a way you can plug in how much you would like to weigh and plug in the time frame you would like to lose the weight in, and it will give you how many calories you should consume in a day.

There is a display on the Fitbit app that lists steps you have taken, how many floors of stairs you have climbed, miles you have walked, calories you have burned, how many active minutes you have spent doing exercise or just moving, and it also lists how much sleep you got the night before. There are badges you can earn for various reasons throughout the week. There is a chart that shows the amount of steps you took each day so you can visually see how much you are moving. Then for each day the amount of steps is listed. Another chart that can be found is a sleep chart. This chart shows how much sleep you are getting and what type of sleep you are getting, from REM sleep, to light sleep, to deep sleep. Remember to make sure you are getting enough sleep, because that is crucial to be successful with weight loss.

Fitbit has a tab called the Fitbit coach. They have mini exercise classes you can click on that give you workouts you can do. This can help you with cardio, flexibility, and building strength. This is great to get a group of friends together and work out or even do alone.

I find Fitbit to be very encouraging and to be a goal-oriented app. It keeps tabs on your progress and lets you know how close you are. It's definitely one of my go-to apps.

Couch to 5K

Couch to 5K is great for those wanting to work up enough endurance to run a 5K. Its goal is to get you off the couch and get you moving, training for your ultimate goal of running a race. This is an eight-week training program where your running will steadily improve over time. It is designed to improve your stamina and endurance with interval training. Starting out, the program has you running minute intervals, and over time working those intervals to longer periods of time. The running will become more challenging, but at the end of the eight weeks you will be more prepared to run a 5K. Even if you don't want to run a 5K, this will help you toward your goal of being healthy.

You can listen to your favorite music, and the program will prompt you when to run and when to walk over the music. Your entire 5K will be directed through your headphones or earbuds until it's complete. The trainer voice tells you when to walk, run, warm up or cool down. You can glance at your phone's screen to know how long you have been running, how much time you have left on that running interval, and how much time you have left on the overall run. It shows the distance you have run, and it allows you to map your runs and track your run routes. At any point you can pause the app if you need to stop along the way. You also have a back button if you want to go to a previous interval or a forward button if you want to skip to the next interval. You can use this app outside or on a treadmill. It can be used in conjunction with any music app. If your goal is to become a runner, this app is for you!

Sworkit Workouts and Fitness Plans

Sworkit is great because it offers workouts for all fitness levels. If you are just starting out or if you have been exercising for a while, Sworkit would be a good fit for you!

It has so much variety in one app! You can choose between strength training, cardio, yoga, and stretching. In the strength-training section, you can choose between these options: full-body workout, upper body workout, core strength, lower body workout, 7-minute workout and rump roaster. The full-body section allows you to pick how many minutes you want to work out, which is perfect if you are in a time crunch. Enjoy your own personal trainer who can focus on strength, cardio, yoga, or stretching. You can also build your own custom workouts or follow guided workout plans. There are so many options that you can switch it up every day to avoid getting bored! Get ready for a leaner, fitter, and stronger you!

5/3/1

This app is built for people wanting to build muscle and strength train! This is a weekly set calculator for Jim Wendler's 5/3/1 strength-building program. The app can be listed in pounds or kilograms. It allows you to keep track of 1RM (Rep Max) or training max for the four compound movements (bench, deadlift, OHP, squat) and achieve set calculations. After one week you can bump up maxes (5/10 lb, 2.5/5 kg.)

I personally haven't used this, but it was strongly recommended by a friend who lifts. After a little research, it looks as if the app is easy to follow and nicely laid out. I wanted to include an app that was easy to use and would help you keep track of how much weight you are lifting. Variety is always nice!

HIIT & Cardio Workout by Fitify

HIIT (high-intensity interval training) is a method that is known for burning fat and calories in a short and intense workout. HIIT is a form of cardiovascular exercise that can include running, bodyweight workouts, yoga, stretching, weightlifting, boxing, sprinting, and cycling. HIIT alternates periods of short, intense anaerobic exercise with less-intense recovery times, cycling back and forth and constantly changing. HIIT sessions can last anywhere from 4 to 30 minutes. These short, intense workouts will give you the best workout in the shortest amount of time.

This app features over 90 bodyweight exercises, four unique workout programs, no equipment needed, voice coach, clear HD video demonstrations, is designed for men and women, young and old, and the best thing is it works offline! You can customize your workouts! Choose your own exercises, duration and rest intervals. It has a great variety of exercises for all muscle groups. This app is easy to navigate and easy to get started.

Zombies, Run!

I am throwing this app in here as something out of the box. It puts a twist on exercise. This app takes place during a zombie apocalypse. The only way to survive is to run! You choose your playlist before you start to run, and in between songs the story unfolds through a series of dynamic radio messages and voice recordings. Your goal is to survive the zombie apocalypse and to save other people by collecting vital supplies like medicine, batteries, and food. This is worth a try if you enjoy things like this. This is strictly a running app and doesn't offer more than just an entertaining storyline, but it's fun and out of the box!

Vacation

How do you vacation, maintain your weight, and still have a great time? Going out of town can often be challenging when trying to lose weight. Don't get discouraged. Follow these simple tips to make life a little easier and still enjoy your time away from home.

1. Figure out where you are going. Once you decide this, the rest will fall into place.

2. Research the area you are visiting. Instead of looking into places to eat, find activities you can do or places you can visit. Check some stuff off of your bucket list.

3. Make new friends or talk to the locals and find new areas to explore.

4. Ask locals or read reviews on places around the town you are visiting to find restaurants. Once you decide where you will be eating, order what you want. Just remember to eat the proper portion size. Either share a plate or get a to-go box. Splurge a

little. You are on vacation! Just stop eating when you start to get full!

5. You might want to consider walking to destinations if they are in walking distance. Burn off some of those additional calories you have acquired.

Vacationing doesn't have to be stressful. Just use common sense. Drink your water and eat small portion sizes. If you feel as if you have overeaten, make time to work out. If you are visiting more than just a couple of days, you will want to do this anyway!

Recently Wes, my husband, and I went to New Orleans, and on the way back we stopped to visit my family. We met up with my mother and brother at a local restaurant (my mother's choice because it was Mother's Day). After sitting down to eat with them, they asked about our trip, but the questions they asked all involved food.

Wes and I only ate at a handful of places, and when we did eat out we shared a plate. Our vacation didn't revolve around food. Our vacation revolved around doing new things and making memories. We went to the bayou and took a boat tour. We went shopping. We walked the streets and watched the street performers, people watched, went to local art galleries, watched the bands, went to a few bars and danced, and we also enjoyed a ton of jazz music. There were so many things we experienced, but the conversation was surrounded by food.

I had never really realized how much food impacted not only my life, but everyone else's as well. It's okay to enjoy your food, but that is what got me in the situation I am in. I LOVE food! I love the smell of it, the taste of it, how it made me feel when I was eating it, but what I didn't love is the toll it took on my body. I was abusing it. There are so many experiences out there that you can enjoy, and you don't always have to turn to food.

Adjust your mindset to where this is a lifestyle change and not your typical diet.

Tips and Tricks
to be a Better You!

-Eat more protein! Eating high-protein foods helps you feel fuller longer!

-Instead of taking the elevator, take the stairs!

-Park at the end of the parking lot and walk to the store. Those extra steps can burn more calories than you realize!

-Figure out what motivates you and get in the right mindset. Stay positive and remain focused.

-Never eat while watching TV or while watching your phone. You really need to listen to your body and stop when you are full.

-Leave yourself notes. If you see something motivational, put it on a sticky note and attach it to the fridge or on the mirror in the bathroom. Leave words of encouragement for yourself or for others!

-Instead of going on a diet, focus on becoming

happier and healthier! Lifestyle changes are long term. Diets aren't. Most people who diet tend to gain more weight back than they were originally. This can be more than frustrating to an individual whose goal is to simply lose the weight.

-Keep fruit in the fridge. Want something sweet? Grab a piece of cold fruit. This will prevent you from looking for something that could sabotage the work you have done that day!

-Don't eat after 8:00 p.m. Never go to bed with a full stomach. Give yourself time to digest before going to bed. This will also help with acid reflux if you deal with that devil!

-Overchew your food! It sounds crazy, but this helps you slow down your eating. The more you chew, the slower you eat. This allows your body time to feel full! It also helps with digestion.

-Brush and floss your teeth after dinner. I do this and it cuts down on my late-night cravings. I am not really sure the reasoning behind this, but maybe it's because it gets my mind ready for bed and I won't eat after I brush my teeth.

-Limit salt intake. Mrs. Dash offers a variety of rubs and seasonings that are sodium free. Sodium can add pounds to a scale just by making you retain water weight.

-Plan all of your meals ahead of time! Whether you are eating at home or eating out, this will prevent you from making poor choices! Do your homework. Know the calorie count! All restaurants these days have their calories posted on their websites and sometimes even on the overhead board behind the register if you are eating fast food. If you are at a sit-down restaurant, the calories are sometimes on the menu. Do the work so you don't regret the decisions you make in your food choices.

-Sugar-free gum, hard candies, and Popsicles are delicious! Take advantage of their deliciousness. Sugar-free tropical Popsicles got me through my toughest decision making! Those things are tasty!

-Avoid processed foods! Eat around the perimeter of the grocery store! You will notice the fruits, vegetables, and meats are all around the outside wall at almost every grocery store! Most processed foods are found in the center of the store because they don't go bad as quickly. Hydrogenated oils are bad for you! They will raise your LDL cholesterol (bad cholesterol.) Shop around the outside walls for the freshest, healthiest foods!

-When eating off of your plate, always eat in this order: protein, vegetables, fruits, then any carbs you might have. Try to keep your carbs to a minimum. Eat slowly, and stop when you are full! Don't forget to drink that water!

-Eat foods high in fiber! Fiber along with adequate amounts of water moves quickly and painlessly through your digestion tract and helps it to function properly.

-Have a positive attitude and don't be a Debbie downer. Nobody likes to be around someone who complains constantly. Have a positive outlook on your situation and on life. This will help you reach your goals and make people want to hang around you!

-STOP EATING WHEN YOU START TO FEEL FULL! There is a lag of time between your stomach and your brain. By the time your brain registers that you are full, you have already eaten too much! So when you start to think you are full, STOP EATING!

-Drink a glass of water BEFORE any meal! This will help you feel fuller faster and will also help you reach your water intake goals.

-Plan family time with activities that make you move! Take your family hiking, walking, skating, play some baseball, soccer, football, tennis, or go swimming. There are so many things you can do to be active. There is no excuse to not be moving!

-Simple fact to losing weight: Moving more and eating less will mean weight loss.

-Take a daily vitamin! This will help with brain function, give you additional energy, and help your metabolism.

-I have heard this time and time again: Never be the smartest person in the room! If you are, you are in the wrong room!

-Don't plan vacations around food! Plan them around activities!

-If your parents or grandparents are still alive, visit them. Call them. Talk to them on a regular basis. They won't be here forever, and you will wish you had more time once they are gone.

-Leave a legacy! Your children should be the most important people in your life. Teach them good habits and make memories with them. They are a direct reflection of YOU! Mold them into good people and instill values and good habits that they can carry on to their children! Trust me. You want to be the cool grandparent!

-Slow cookers are your friends. They can save you time and money. Look up healthy recipes online! There are so many to choose from!

-Someone is always watching, and it's usually those little people who call you Mommy or Daddy. Be the example, lead the way, and show them how to live a healthy lifestyle so one day they can pass it on to their children. If your grandparents were overweight, your parents are overweight, and you are overweight, chances are your children are, too. Break the cycle and be the generation that takes control. Nobody is going to do it for you. Tough love is sometimes all you have to give, and this is tough love!

-Share a meal and order water at restaurants! Take the money you would have spent on the additional meal and drink and put it in a jar! If you are a family on the go like we are, that money you will save will add up quickly!

-Take time out for quiet! This is a necessity! Everyone needs downtime. It is important to allow yourself time to recuperate, and it helps with your sanity!

-Exercise. Even if you don't feel like exercising, make yourself. Once you are finished, you will feel great and you will be proud of yourself.

-If you are able, find an exercise partner. It makes exercising more enjoyable and the time will pass more quickly!

-Invest in yourself. There is always something you can improve and something you want to learn. Take the time to improve yourself! There is only one YOU!

-Get comfortable being uncomfortable! You need to step outside your comfort zone and do things you have never done before. Once you do this, it will open a new world of possibilities for you.

-Love more and forgive often. Don't carry around anger. Once you forgive, a burden will be lifted off of your shoulders.

-Learn. Take action, and enjoy the ride! Every day should be a new adventure!

Simple Formula for Living

Rules to Live By

-Put your phone down! Enjoy the moment.

-Live beneath your means.

-Be grateful.

-Save money.

-Encourage others. You never know the struggles they are going through.

-Do what you say you are going to do when you say you are going to do it.

-Return everything you borrow.

-Get out of debt.

-Do something nice for someone.

-Never go to bed angry.

-Always tell your loved ones that you love them.

-Admit it when you make a mistake.

-Stop blaming other people.

-Stand up to bullies.

-Be present.

-Read more.

-Write handwritten thank you notes.

-If given the chance, dance in the rain.

-Do something nice for someone and try not to get caught doing it.

-Listen more.

-Talk less.

-Love like you don't get a tomorrow.

-Give clothes not worn to charity or the homeless.

-Strive for excellence, not perfection.

-Don't argue. It's pointless.

-Get organized.

-Be kind to unkind people.

-Be a friend.

-Use good manners.

-Be on time. Don't make excuses.

-Let someone cut ahead of you in line.

-Stand up for the innocent.

-Don't complain.

-Be strong.

-Be thankful.

-Be positive.

-Be humble.

-Realize and accept life isn't fair.

-Live in the present.

-Know when to keep your mouth shut.

-Go an entire day without criticizing someone.

-Keep an open mind.

-Be an inspiration to others!

-Improvement is progress, one pound at a time.

-Knowledge is power!

-Learn from the past. Plan for the future.

The Follow-Through

Any great salesman will say this is the most important step in making a sale. I would have to agree. The follow-through is what happens when it's all said and done. It's the final step to reaching out to someone to let them know they are being thought about. It's the final nail in the coffin for a sale. I have mentioned this a few times in this book. It's simple: Do what you say you are going to do and follow through with it. Push yourself and hold yourself accountable. Once you follow though, you will be well on your way to living a healthy lifestyle. Once you hit your goal, you must maintain! Don't revert back to old, nasty habits. Love yourself! Just remember: Nothing tastes as good as healthy feels!

YOU GOT THIS!

I hope this book helps you along your personal journey. If you are ready to put these tips and tricks to work, you may be interested in my Dump the Plump planner/journal. This provides a way to track your results and hold yourself accountable. There is no wrong or right way to lose weight. I am not here to tell you that my way works better than others. We all have a common goal, let's support one another and love ourselves while doing it! Just always remember- You are loved, and you are worth it! Thanks for reading!